P9-DWM-964

DAMAGE NOTED
Front
corner
torn center
bottom

The Complete

Get That Job!

A quick and easy guide with worksheets

CONTRA COSTA COUNTY
JUVENILE HALL LIBRARY

PLEASE DO NOT WRITE
IN THIS BOOK!!!
WE WILL COPY ANY
PAGE YOU WOULD LIKE,
JUST ASK THE
LIBRARIANS. THANKS!

New Readers Press

Acknowledgments

Thanks to the following people for their contribution to the content of *Get That Job!*: James Gourley, Pennsylvania New Reader Representative; John Zickefoose, READ NOW!, Corona Public Library, Corona, California; Joanna Miller, Education Coordinator, Southerners for Economic Justice, Durham, North Carolina; Toni Cordell, New Reader Leadership Coordinator, Laubach Literacy; and J. William McVey, Director, Laubach Literacy Center for Workforce Education.

The Complete Get That Job!
ISBN 1-56420-233-X
Copyright © 2001
Jurg Oppliger, New Readers Press
Division of ProLiteracy Worldwide
1320 Jamesville Ave., Syracuse, New York 13210

All rights reserved. No part of this book may be reproduced or transmitted in any form or by any means, electronic or mechanical, including photocopying, recording, or by any information storage and retrieval system, without permission in writing from the publisher.

Printed in the United States of America
9 8 7 6 5

Director of Acquisitions and Development: Christina Jagger
Content Editor: Judi Lauber
Copy Editor: Terrie Lipke
Production Director: Deborah Christiansen
Designer: Kimbrly Koennecke
Cover Designer: Kimbrly Koennecke
Illustrators: Linda Tiff, Luciana Mallozzi
Production Specialist: Shelagh Clancy

All proceeds from the sale of New Readers Press materials support literacy programs in the United States and worldwide.

Contents

Introduction

You want to find a job. Maybe you want to change jobs. Perhaps you're in school or unemployed. Whatever you're doing now, planning your job search can help you find a new job more quickly. And it can improve your chances of getting a job you like.

This book is for all job seekers. It shows how to use your basic skills and knowledge to find a good job.

If you take the actions this book suggests, you can

- decide what you can do well
- identify your job search goals
- pick the best way to look for the job you want
- write effective resumes and cover letters
- prepare for job interviews
- find a good job
- get off to a good start in your new job

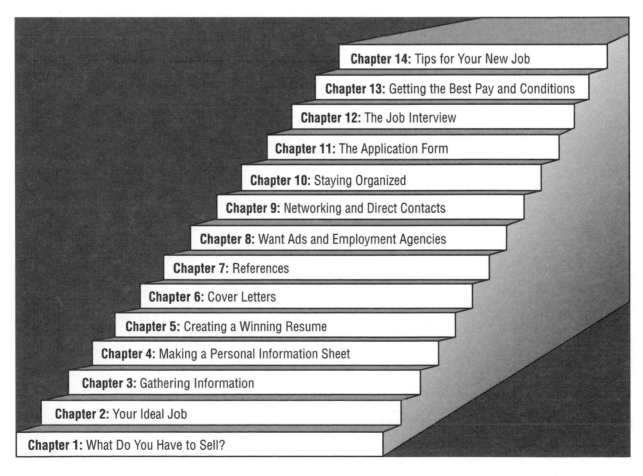

Chapter 14: Tips for Your New Job

Chapter 13: Getting the Best Pay and Conditions

Chapter 12: The Job Interview

Chapter 11: The Application Form

Chapter 10: Staying Organized

Chapter 9: Networking and Direct Contacts

Chapter 8: Want Ads and Employment Agencies

Chapter 7: References

Chapter 6: Cover Letters

Chapter 5: Creating a Winning Resume

Chapter 4: Making a Personal Information Sheet

Chapter 3: Gathering Information

Chapter 2: Your Ideal Job

Chapter 1: What Do You Have to Sell?

This book has 14 chapters (see page 5). Each chapter describes one step of a successful job search.

How to Use This Book

You will get the most out of this book if you go through it twice:

- First read it through quickly without doing the exercises and activities. This gives you an overview of the job search process.
- Then work through the book more slowly, doing the exercises and activities.

How Soon Can I Find a Job?

There's no way to know for sure how long your job search will take. It can take a lot of time and hard work.

To succeed, you may have to contact many companies.* The more contacts you make, the sooner you are likely to find a job.

Finding a job also takes luck. If you're lucky, you could find work within a week or two. But for most people, it takes much longer.

Sometimes, 100 people may apply for a single job. Only one person will be hired. That means 99 won't. Be prepared to apply for many jobs before you find the one you want. Don't become discouraged.

This book gives you a recipe for a successful job search. Now, get that job!

---

* In this book, the word *company* is used to refer to any workplace. It could be a company, an institution (school, hospital, etc.), a small business, or another kind of organization.

The Complete

Chapter 1

What Do You Have to Sell?

Looking for a job is selling yourself—your experience, your skills, your knowledge, and your ability to work with others. How do you know what you have to sell? Spend some time thinking about these questions:

- What do I like to do?
- What are my strongest points?
- What can I do best?
- What do I know best?
- What sort of job should I look for?

This is a good way to start identifying your skills. Next, look at some areas in more detail.

What You Like Doing

When you like your job, you'll do it much better and you'll be happier. Consider what you really like to do at work and what bothers or frustrates you.

Think about your most recent job and what you like best and least about it. Maybe you like being proud of your company's product. Maybe you're frustrated because you think your pay is too low.

The following questions can help you figure out what you like and want to do:

- What motivates me and makes me proud of my work?
- What are my favorite interests outside of work?
- What size workplace suits me best?
- Do I like to work with people?
- Do I want to work alone or in a group?
- Do I like being part of a team?
- Do I want to be responsible for other people's work, or just my own?
- Do I like being in charge?
- Do I enjoy helping people?
- Do I enjoy gathering information?
- Do I enjoy using machinery?

- Do I like meeting many new people?
- Do I like to work with my hands?
- Do I like being responsible for money?
- Do I like making a lot of phone calls?
- Do I like sitting a lot at work?
- Do I like to organize things?
- Do I like to solve problems?
- Do I like to work carefully and accurately?
- Do I like working unusual hours?
- Do I like working flexible hours?
- Do I like working lots of overtime?
- Do I want to move to a new area?
- Do I want to work for myself?

The chart below shows how someone could list job likes and dislikes.

Job Likes and Dislikes

In my most recent job, I like
- talking to customers and helping them make good choices
- displaying products for sale in an attractive way
- helping to choose cosmetics and shampoos to stock

In other jobs, I liked
- close relations with the owner and my coworkers
- small size of the salon
- short distance from home to work

In my most recent job, I don't like
- closing the salon in the evening
- filling out daily tally sheets
- responsibility for cash

In other jobs, I didn't like
- low salary
- being one of many salespeople

I Like / I Don't Like

Think about your current job and jobs you had in the past. List job features that you like and that you do not like. Be specific.

	I Like	I Don't Like
Tasks		
Qualities of My Supervisor		
Level of Responsibility		
Salary and Benefits		
Working Conditions (hours, location, working alone or with others, etc.)		
Opportunity to Advance		

Strong and Weak Points

Think about your strong points. What character traits do you have that an employer may need? Are you a leader? Good with people? Always on time? Your strong points are part of what you have to sell.

You also need to know your weak points, so that you don't take a job you don't like or can't do. What limits the work you can do? Do you need detailed instructions? Do you need quiet to concentrate?

Some qualities might be strong points for one job but weak points for another. Are you a quiet person? That would be a strong point for a library job. But it would be a weak point for selling cars.

The chart below shows a sample list. When you make your own list, try to include at least six strong points.

Strong and Weak Points	
My strong points	**My weak points**
precise	a little slow
careful	too quick to give in
hardworking	not a natural leader
patient	
reliable	
good team worker	
forgiving	
adaptable	

Here are some strong points for many kinds of jobs. Do any of them apply to you?

adaptable	fair	kind	quiet
calm	flexible	loyal	reliable
careful	forgiving	methodical	self-confident
caring	friendly	orderly	serious
committed	good-natured	outgoing	sincere
controlled	hardworking	patient	strong
cooperative	helpful	persistent	talkative
creative	honest	pleasant	team player
dependable	independent	polite	thoughtful
energetic	intelligent	precise	well-groomed

Think about your character traits. Then list your strong and weak points below. Try to include two strong points for every weak point. Be specific. Put a star next to any that are especially important.

My Strong Points   **My Weak Points**

_____   _____

_____   _____

_____   _____

_____   _____

_____   _____

_____   _____

_____   _____

_____   _____

_____

_____

_____

_____

_____

Now, talk to at least three people who know you well. Ask them what they think are your strong and weak points. If you agree, add new items to your lists.

Skills and Knowledge

Next, think about the skills and knowledge you already have. Which could help you get a job?

If you're an office worker, your job skills and knowledge could include

- word processing
- knowing several software applications
- accounting
- using the telephone
- setting up filing systems
- running photocopiers and fax machines

When you think about your skills and knowledge, don't limit yourself to what you've done on the job. You may have learned to manage your time well by running a household. You may have learned teamwork by being on a volunteer committee. Maybe you build models as a hobby—you've learned to work neatly and carefully. These skills and knowledge are probably selling points too.

The chart below shows an example of how a person could list skills and knowledge.

Skills and Knowledge

I can

restock shelves
do inventory control
handle electric and
   electronic cash registers
do daily tally sheets
train people (as
   baseball coach)
do first aid and CPR
raise children

I know

common food brands
bar code reading
Mexican currency
Spanish

When you make your own list, try to include all the specific items you can think of.

Skills Inventory

List your skills. Try to list at least one skill in each category. List more wherever possible. Use strong action verbs. Explain why the skills are important in a job.

	Skills	Why Important
Skills from Work Experience		
Skills from School or Training		
Skills from Volunteer Activities		
Skills from Hobbies, Recreation, or Clubs		
Skills from Home and Family Responsibilities		

Success Stories

By now, you have some idea of what you have to sell to an employer. There's one more factor that can help you go out and sell yourself: self-confidence. If people see that you believe in yourself, they're more likely to believe in you too.

You might want to try writing your success stories. Your success stories can help in three ways:

- They boost your self-confidence and remind you of what you can do well.
- You can use them in your resume to show what you can do.
- You can mention them in job interviews.

It's effective to tell a success story in three parts:

1. The problem: the situation that you faced
2. The action: what you did to solve the problem or change the situation
3. The result: what came out of your action

Anything you are proud of is worth writing up. Try to think of more than one success story. Think of things you did well in the past. Remember when your boss, your coworkers, or a family member complimented you. Include situations on and off the job.

Page 15 shows an example of a success story.

Success Story

1. **Problem** In our manufacturing operation, we shared some tools. It was often a problem to find the tool you needed.
2. **Action** I mounted hooks on the wall for all the tools to be hung. Each worker got one metal name tag to be put on the hook when taking a tool.
3. **Result** Each worker had only one tool at a time, and the tools could easily be found. We cut out many hours of searching.

Success Stories

Try writing one or two success stories of your own. Continue on separate paper if you need to.

Success Story 1
1. Problem:
2. Action:
3. Result:

Success Story 2
1. Problem:
2. Action:
3. Result:

Chapter 2
Your Ideal Job

In Chapter 1, you thought about what you can do and what you like to do. Using that information, you can decide what kind of a job you want.

Try to describe your ideal job. What would make a job perfect for you?

You may not find a job that's perfect in every detail—few people do. But you can compare possible jobs to your ideal. Are they close enough? If not, one of those jobs may not satisfy you. You could soon be looking for work again.

Here is how someone's description of an ideal job might look.

My Ideal Job

Job Description

I want a cooking job. I'd like to work with the head chef at a hotel so that I can improve my cooking skills.

Job Conditions

- work mornings and early afternoons (so that I can be home with my daughter in the evenings)
- located not more than 40 minutes from my home
- friendly coworkers

Pay and Benefits

I need to make at least as much as on my last job. If possible, I'd prefer to make 10 percent more.

I want to have these benefits:
- health insurance for me and my daughter
- retirement plan
- two weeks' vacation

Other Issues

- no overtime

Use your answers to the activities on pages 9 and 13. Think about what features you want in a job. Think about what features you need, such as hours or benefits. Write a description of your ideal job.

Job Description

I want a job in the _____ field. I want a job in which I can _____

_____

I want the chance to _____

because _____

The kind of company I'm looking for is _____

Job Conditions

I would like to work in a place that is _____

I'd like to work the hours of _____ because _____

_____

I'm hoping for coworkers who _____

Pay and Benefits

I want to make a salary of _____ , but I need to make at least _____

I want a job that offers these benefits: _____

I need them because _____

Other Issues

I want a job in which I don't have to _____

because _____

These things are also important to me: _____

_____

Long-Term Goals

Most often, a job search is treated as a short-term effort. You need a job right away so you can pay the bills.

But at the same time, it's good to think ahead. Where would you like to be 10 years from now? Think of both work and personal goals. To get there, what kind of job should you look for now?

Here is an example of someone's 10-year goals.

10-Year Goals

Work goals

Kind of job: I want my own bicycle repair shop.
Income needed: enough to support a family and buy
   a house

Personal goals that affect my job needs

- stay in this area near my family
- be active in the community
- be married and have children
- own my own home

When you write up your own 10-year goals, take your time. Put it aside and come back to it with fresh thoughts. Talk it over with your spouse or partner, if you have one. Make sure you plan to help you both reach your goals.

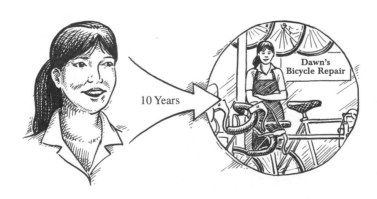

10 Years

Dawn's Bicycle Repair

The Complete

Chapter 3
Gathering Information

You've thought about

- what you have to sell an employer
- your special skills and knowledge
- what you like to do
- what kind of job you want

Now it's time to start networking and making contacts to help you in your job search. It's also time to think about where you might like to work.

Networking List

About two-thirds of job openings in the U.S. are never advertised. Instead, employers hire

- people they know
- people who are recommended
- people who ask for a job at the right time

How do you find out about these "hidden" job openings? The answer is networking.

Networking means getting the word out that you are looking for a job. Think about everyone you know who might be a useful contact. Look at the ideas on page 20. Useful contacts are people who can

- recommend you to an employer
- let you know about job openings
- give you information about a line of work that interests you
- give you information about a company that interests you

As you think of people, start writing them down on a networking list. Page 20 shows how part of a list might look. When you make your own list, include anyone you can think of.

Start your list now by doing the activity on page 21. Every day, think about adding to your list. This helps make sure that you don't forget anybody who could help you.

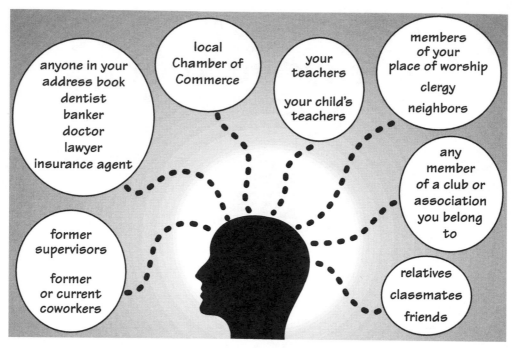

Networking

Networking List

Name: Jim Buzzell   Phone: 555-6543 (H)
Notes: wife Heidi, son Peter
Question: May I use you as a reference?

Name: Kathy Bardolino   Phone: 555-7890 (W)
Question: Are there any sales jobs open where you work?

Name: Bill Smolka   Phone: 555-5457 (W)
Notes: my boss 1985–94
Question: Do you think with my skills I'd be good at sales?

Build Your Network

List your key networking contacts. Include the person's full name. Record the best phone number to call the person. Mark it *H* for "home" or *W* for "work." On the *Notes* line, list such things as the person's company, job, or title, or who referred you to that person. For each contact, write at least one key question you want to ask.

1. Name: _____ Phone: _____

Notes: _____

Question: _____

2. Name: _____ Phone: _____

Notes: _____

Question: _____

3. Name: _____ Phone: _____

Notes: _____

Question: _____

4. Name: _____ Phone: _____

Notes: _____

Question: _____

5. Name: _____ Phone: _____

Notes: _____

Question: _____

6. Name: _____ Phone: _____

Notes: _____

Question: _____

Company List

It's also a good idea to start a company list right away. This is a list of companies you think could use somebody with your skills, and that you would like to work for.

Looking where you live

If you want a job in the area where you already live, there are many ways to identify companies.

- **Think of companies you know.** These may include your present and past employers, as well as companies that are in the same business. Think also about your employer's customers and suppliers. Do they hire people with your skills? Consider the companies where your friends and relatives work, too.
- **Look around you.** Make note of signs and of trucks that drive by.
- **Remember to check the Internet.** It's a good place to find lists of businesses in your area, as well as information about many companies and industries.

- **Read the ads in local newspapers and magazines.** Look at ads for products or services that interest you. Would you like to work for any of those companies? Look at employment ads too, even if you're not interested in the job. You can always use the companies' names and addresses to write for a job that you do want.
- **Use the telephone yellow pages.** Look for the kind of companies that might need employees with your skills. Use your imagination. If you want to work around cars, look under such listings as "Automobiles," "Mufflers," "Brake Service," "Motorcycles," "Tractors," "Trailers," "Transmissions," "Truck Dealers," "Truck Repair," "Trucking," and so on. If you want to work in personal care, look under such listings as "Hairdressers," "Beauty Salons," "Nail Salons," "Weight Control Services," and so on.
- **Don't ignore small businesses.** Companies with 20 or fewer employees create most of the new jobs in the United States.

Looking in other areas

If you plan to relocate, your local library can help you. You'll find references—both electronic and print—that list companies in other cities. You can look for a specific town or county, or for a specific industry.

People working at the library can help you find the best resources. One of the most useful is the Internet. It has information about industries and many individual companies. You can also find information about various cities, careers, and other job research. Many libraries will let you access the Internet.

These resources can also be helpful:
- *Moody's Industry Review* (a three- to six-page report published every two weeks)
- *Thomas Register of American Manufacturers* (30 volumes with information on 140,000 manufacturing companies, products, and services)
- *The Career Guide: Dun's Employment Opportunities Directory* (with details about more than 5,000 U.S. companies and other job research information. Updated every year.)

Making your company list

As you select companies, add them to your company list. Try to identify a contact person at each company too. This could be someone from your networking list. It could also be the person in charge of the area you want to work in.

The sample on page 24 shows what a company list might look like.

Company List

Company name	Contact person's name	Remarks
The Freedel Corp.	Jack Dewey	production manager
The Wonder Co.		battery maker
Doolittle, Inc.	Marisa Lopez	printed circuits

It's best to treat your company list as you do your networking list. Start it early, and add to it every day.

Company List

Begin listing companies where you'd like to work. Check the tips on pages 22–23 for ideas on where to look. Use extra sheets of paper if you need to.

Company name	Contact person's name	Remarks

Chapter 4
Making a Personal Information Sheet

You've done the early work for a job search. You know what kind of work you can do. You've thought about what kind of job you'd like and where you want to work. And you've started finding contacts and learning about companies. Now you can begin to get ready to sell yourself to an employer.

When you're job hunting, many employers will ask you for a resume and a list of references. And most want you to fill out a job application form. You want to be prepared. Your first step is to gather all the information you'll need. You can put it together into a personal information sheet (see pages 26–27).

When you fill out the personal information sheet, answer all the questions that apply to you. Don't worry yet about what an employer will think. This sheet is for your use only. No one but you needs to see it.

Make sure all the information on your sheet is correct. Check names, addresses, and phone numbers. If you're not sure about a date or a fact, look it up if you can.

Under "Education and Training," be sure to list all the schools you've attended. Include job training classes if they were at least three days long.

Under "Work Experience," list all the jobs you've had. List them in order, with the most recent one first.

Under "References," list people who know your work well. They can be supervisors, coworkers, or friends. Don't use relatives as references, though. Be sure to include a daytime phone number for each reference.

After you finish, keep your sheet to refer to. It will help you write a resume. It will also help you fill out job application forms.

You may want to make several copies. That way, you can keep one copy in a safe place. And you can carry another copy with you on your job hunt. Then, you'll have all your important information at your fingertips.

Personal Information Sheet

Fill out this sheet. Answer all the questions that apply to you. Answer as completely as possible. Use this information when you write your resume and when you fill out application forms.

Personal Data

Full name: _____

Address: _____

Telephone: _____ (home) _____ (work)

Social Security number: _____

U.S. citizen? _____ Yes _____ No

If no, Alien Registration number: _____

U.S. military service? _____ Yes _____ No

If yes, what branch? _____

Dates: From _____ To _____ Last rank: _____

Have you ever been convicted of a felony? _____ Yes _____ No

If yes, give details: _____

Any physical or mental disabilities that would prevent you from performing a job?

_____ Yes _____ No   If yes, explain: _____

Machines and equipment you can operate: _____

_____

Work desired: _____ Full-time _____ Part-time

If part-time: _____ days per week _____ hours per day

Available for: _____ Evening work _____ Weekend work _____ Shift work

Willing to work overtime if necessary? _____ Yes _____ No

When are you available to start work? _____

Education and Training

School: _____ Location: _____

Dates attended: _____ Graduated? _____ Yes _____ No

Degree or certificate: _____ Subject(s) studied: _____

School: _____ Location: _____

Dates attended: _____ Graduated? _____ Yes _____ No

Degree or certificate: _____ Subject(s) studied: _____

Work Experience

Company: _____ Phone number: _____

Address: _____ Dates employed: _____

Job title: _____ Supervisor: _____

Duties: _____

Salary: Starting _____ Ending _____ Reason for leaving: _____

Company: _____ Phone number: _____

Address: _____ Dates employed: _____

Job title: _____ Supervisor: _____

Duties: _____

Salary: Starting _____ Ending _____ Reason for leaving: _____

References

Name	Relationship	Phone number(s)
_____	_____	_____
_____	_____	_____
_____	_____	_____

Chapter 5
Creating a Winning Resume

A resume is a one-page sheet that tells an employer about your skills, training, and experience. Making a resume is an important early step in a job search. For some jobs, your resume is your first contact with an employer. It should make employers want to interview you. For other jobs, your first major contact with an employer will be an interview. You can review your resume to prepare for the interview.

Creating a winning resume takes two steps:

1. Decide what information to include and how to present it.
2. Have the resume word-processed or typed and then copied.

Write the Resume

Resumes can be written in different ways to highlight your strengths. Many people highlight previous work experience. This is a good idea if your experience shows what you have to sell.

But maybe you don't have much work experience. Or maybe you want to change to a different kind of job. Organize your resume so that an employer can quickly see what skills and knowledge you have to offer.

Your resume should not mention age, race, religion, family status, or ethnicity. Employers are not supposed to use this information in hiring. You should also leave out political views and health concerns.

Pages 30–31 show two examples of strong resumes.

When you write your own resume, take into account the lists of your strong points, skills, and knowledge from Chapter 1. Your success stories can also help you. They'll remind you of accomplishments you can include.

Tailor the resume to move you toward your ideal job from Chapter 2. Use any information you need from the personal information sheet you made in Chapter 4. Write everything that comes to mind. You can always revise the resume later.

Use action words to describe what you've done. This helps highlight your skills and successes.

Not as good:

". . . was in charge of hiring all support staff"

Better:

". . . hired all support staff"

Here are examples of words that work well in resumes:

arranged	developed	launched	prepared	solved
assigned	directed	led	reduced	supervised
built	hired	managed	saved	tested
created	improved	organized	served	trained
designed	increased	planned	sold	won

RESUME

DO's	DON'Ts
+ Use action verbs, direct words, and short sentences.	— Don't list your hobbies, unless they relate to the job.
+ List first the skills and experience that will most impress a particular employer.	— Don't list references.
+ Make it easy to read. Important information should stand out clearly. Most employers will spend only about a minute reading it the first time.	— Don't list past salaries or what you hope to make.
+ Customize your resume to the jobs you want to apply for.	— Don't give reasons for leaving any job.
+ Stick to one page. Use good quality white or off-white paper.	— Don't include a photo.
+ Be sure it's clean and neat with no spelling errors.	— Don't mention your age, race, religion, family status, nationality, or ethnicity.
+ Check that you've included all your positive qualities and successes.	— Don't be general or unfocused.
+ Send a cover letter if you mail your resume (see Chapter 6).	— Don't handwrite.

Use the resume diagram on page 32 as a guide. Be sure to include information for each of the five main sections.

After you write your first draft, it's good to wait at least one day, then read your resume again. Have you forgotten anything important? Did you include anything that is not relevant? Change anything you don't like.

Tyrone Thomas   123 Sea Road   Uptown, NY 12345   (518) 555-7891

Summary

Energetic, hard-working individual seeking entry-level position with a computer manufacturer. A responsible and reliable person who enjoys contributing to a team effort and creating a good working environment. Has a wide range of manual and office support skills.

Skills and Experience

Maintenance

- Carpenter's helper
  - painted interior walls
  - measured and cut lumber
  - helped with framing
  - operated power tools (saws, drills, sanders)
- Basic home maintenance
  - rewired lamps
  - repaired plumbing and appliances
  - built shelves
- Completed classes in
  - electronics (built a TV scrambler from a circuit board)
  - architectural drafting
  - basic carpentry

Office Support

- Assisted in inventory control and priced merchandise at Robert's Market
- Cashiered at Robert's, computing and handling large sums of money
- Answered phones as needed
- Completed class in marketing, including product development and simulated marketing strategies

Computer Knowledge

- Basic understanding of Windows environment and a variety of software applications

Work History

- June 1998 to present, Stock Clerk/Cashier, Robert's Market, Binghamton, NY
- Summer 1997, Valet Parking Assistant, Melo Country Club, Woodside, NY

Education

- Woodside High School, Woodside, NY, 1998
- Binghamton Junior College, Binghamton, NY. Currently taking night classes in computers and business administration.

Luz Rodriguez
29 Brighton Avenue
Farmingville, NY 11738
(516) 555-2178

Summary

Honest, reliable, and productive worker seeking position as supermarket assistant manager trainee. Nine years' experience in grocery industry as head clerk, checker, and cashier. Excellent reputation with customers as competent, knowledgeable, and helpful.

Work History

1992–present, retail clerk, COOP Supermarket, Woodstock, NY

Customer Service

Developed a reputation for excellent customer service by
- smiling and making eye contact
- greeting customers in a friendly manner and giving them full attention
- taking time to answer a question or find someone else who could

Served as product expert, directing customers to
- unusual spices and ingredients
- ethnic foods
- gourmet items

Increased sales and customer satisfaction in the higher-profit natural foods department by advising customers on bulk alternatives to name-brand items

Supervisory

As head clerk, managed front end of the store
- prepared daily schedules for up to 18 clerks to assure best coverage
- assigned staff to cover peak hours and continuous stocking

Trained new clerks

Administrative

Balanced checker's cash drawer with consistently high level of accuracy

As office cashier for one year
- accurately balanced books and deposits
- answered phones
- prepared daily and monthly sales reports
- made deposits
- processed returned checks

Previous Work History

1991, buyer's assistant, Capwell's, Hartford, NY

1986–1991, manager's assistant, Rusann's Clothing Store, Spokane, WA

Education

Business classes, 1992, Hartford Community College

Military Service

1984–1985, U.S. Air Force

Your name, address, and phone number.

Be sure employers can reach you here.
If you have an e-mail address, include that too.

Job history and job strengths.

List your previous jobs. For each, include all or some of the following:

- name and location of the company
- what the company does, if it is not well known
- the dates you worked there
- your tasks and responsibilities
- one or two successes (Think back on your success stories.)

If you have not had a job before, list your skills, knowledge, and any training you have had. Focus on things that will impress an employer.

Luz Rodriguez
29 Brighton Avenue
Farmingville, NY 11738
(516) 555-2178

Summary

Honest, reliable, and productive worker seeking position as supermarket assistant manager trainee. Nine years' experience in grocery industry as head clerk, checker, and cashier. Excellent reputation with customers as competent, knowledgeable, and helpful.

Work History

1992–present, retail clerk, COOP Supermarket, Woodstock, NY

Customer Service

Developed a reputation for excellent customer service by
- smiling and making eye contact
- greeting customers in a friendly manner and giving them full attention
- taking time to answer a question or find someone else who could

Served as product expert, directing customers to
- unusual spices and ingredients
- ethnic foods
- gourmet items

Increased sales and customer satisfaction in the higher-profit natural foods department by advising customers on bulk alternatives to name-brand items

Supervisory

As head clerk, managed front end of the store
- prepared daily schedules for up to 18 clerks to assure best coverage
- assigned staff to cover peak hours and continuous stocking

Trained new clerks

Administrative

Balanced checker's cash drawer with consistently high level of accuracy

As office cashier for one year
- accurately balanced books and deposits
- answered phones
- prepared daily and monthly sales reports
- made deposits
- processed returned checks

Previous Work History

1991, buyer's assistant, Capwell's, Hartford, NY

1986–1991, manager's assistant, Rusann's Clothing Store, Spokane, WA

Education

Business classes, 1992, Hartford Community College

Military Service

1984–1985, U.S. Air Force

Summary.

These two to six lines describe your strengths and job goals. This paragraph is important, so spend some time on it. Call attention to your strongest selling points.

Education.

If you've attended high school, don't include your elementary school. If you've gone to college, don't list your high school.

Other information.

For example:

- any languages you speak, read, or write other than English
- licenses or certificates related to the job
- time spent in the U.S. military
- successes in sports or clubs, if related to the job
- hobbies, if related to the job
- volunteer work

Mention only things that may interest an employer.

Prepare the Final Version

Now you're ready to put the final touches on your resume. These touches make your resume look polished and professional. It will be ready to open doors for you.

The final version of your resume should be word-processed or typed. If you can't do it yourself, have someone else do it for you. It is worth paying for word processing if you need to.

Use the checklist on page 34 to help you check your resume. Then show your resume to one or two people whose judgment you trust. Ask if they would interview you after reading your resume. If they wouldn't, ask why not. See if you can change anything to make your resume work better.

You now have a resume that will give an employer a clear idea of who you are and what you have to sell.

Resume Checklist

Check your resume. Have you followed these guidelines? If part of your resume needs more work, revise it. Then check the resume again.

Yes   **Needs Work**

_____   _____   **1.** Put name, address, phone number(s), and e-mail address (if you have one) at top.

_____   _____   **2.** Use action verbs and precise words.

_____   _____   **3.** Organize information so that it is easy to read.

_____   _____   **4.** Summarize key strengths and career objective or job goal.

_____   _____   **5.** List work experiences, skills, and education or training.

_____   _____   **6.** List licenses or certificates related to the job you want.

_____   _____   **7.** Highlight important qualifications related to the job you want.

_____   _____   **8.** Give details of major accomplishments. Include numbers if possible.

_____   _____   **9.** Customize information to fit a particular job.

_____   _____   **10.** Include relevant skills from activities outside of paid work.

_____   _____   **11.** Include job-related awards or honors.

_____   _____   **12.** Include all important information, but keep it brief.

_____   _____   **13.** Don't include salary requirements or past salaries.

_____   _____   **14.** Don't list personal data such as age, sex, or marital status.

_____   _____   **15.** Carefully check spelling, punctuation, and capitalization.

_____   _____   **16.** Make sure all information is accurate.

_____   _____   **17.** Keep resume to one page if possible.

_____   _____   **18.** Use white or off-white paper for the resume.

Chapter 6
Cover Letters

For many jobs, you will need to mail your resume. When you send your resume to a company, you should also include a cover letter.

The cover letter is a good chance to sell yourself to an employer. It should be

- brief—no more than one page long
- neatly typed, with no typos or other errors
- tailored to the job you want
- addressed to a person by name
- upbeat and interesting
- on paper that matches your resume, if possible

A good cover letter includes these features:

- your address
- your phone number, including area code
- the date
- inside address
- a greeting
- an introduction (Mention the job, how you heard about it, and that you think you would do well.)
- a body (Tell why you would do well, and show your interest in the company.)
- a conclusion (Ask for an interview, and thank the employer.)
- your signature
- the word *Enclosure* (showing that your resume is enclosed)

Teresa Ippolito
127 North Road
Upville, FL 34062
(407) 555-1357

March 19, 2000

Ms. Doris Miller
Human Resources
Clark's Department Store
PO Box 123
Upville, FL 34062

Dear Ms. Miller:

I am applying for the job of security officer advertised in today's paper. I believe I meet all the requirements and would do a good job for you.

I am over 20 years old. I am physically fit and play basketball regularly in a community league. I have no criminal record, and my driver's license is clean. I have been driving for 10 years, two years as a school bus driver.

My former employers will confirm that I am reliable and conscientious. I am available for full-time work on any shift, including evenings or weekends.

My resume is enclosed. I'll call you early next week to see if we can arrange an interview. I look forward to meeting with you. Thank you for your consideration.

Sincerely,

Teresa Ippolito

Teresa Ippolito

Enclosure

Suppose someone wants to respond to this newspaper ad:

SECURITY OFFICER
Full-time position. Applicants to be over 20 years old, physically fit, with a valid driver's license and no criminal record. Send resume to Doris Miller, Human Resources, Clark's Department Store, PO Box 123, Upville, FL 34062.

A cover letter should tell why the applicant would do well in the job. The ad says that applicants should meet four requirements:

- be over 20 years old
- be physically fit
- have a valid driver's license
- have no criminal record

The cover letter should say that the writer meets all these requirements. It should also mention anything else that would suit the writer for this job.

Page 37 shows an example of a strong cover letter responding to this ad.

Page 38 shows another example of a cover letter. The writer is interested in an office job. He heard about it from someone at the company.

When you write your own cover letter, use the checklist on page 39. It will help you create an effective letter. The checklist notes items that should be in your letter. It also mentions items you should leave out.

Teresa Ippolito
127 North Road
Upville, FL 34062
(407) 555-1357

March 19, 2000

Ms. Doris Miller
Human Resources
Clark's Department Store
PO Box 123
Upville, FL 34062

Dear Ms. Miller:

I am applying for the job of security officer advertised in today's paper. I believe
I meet all the requirements and would do a good job for you.

I am over 20 years old. I am physically fit and play basketball regularly in a
community league. I have no criminal record, and my driver's license is clean.
I have been driving for 10 years, two years as a school bus driver.

My former employers will confirm that I am reliable and conscientious. I am
available for full-time work on any shift, including evenings or weekends.

My resume is enclosed. I'll call you early next week to see if we can arrange an
interview. I look forward to meeting with you. Thank you for your consideration.

Sincerely,

Teresa Ippolito

Teresa Ippolito

Enclosure

John Sewell
947 Millers Lane
Mayville, NH 07421
(603) 555-6776

May 17, 2000

Mr. J.H. Walsh
Director of Human Resources
Quality Corporation
2121 North Avenue
South Mayville, NH 07407

Dear Mr. Walsh:

Agnes Jones, sales manager at Quality Corporation, suggested that I write to you. She told me that a job for an administrative assistant is open in the sales department. I believe I have the background to help keep the department organized and running smoothly.

I have been working for five years as an administrative assistant at Classic, Inc. I regularly use word processing, spreadsheet, and database programs and other computer software. I type and format all letters and internal memos. I also manage customer information and prepare invoices. I recently reorganized the customer records and computer files for easier use. I have also trained six staff members in word processing.

I feel I would fit in well at Quality Corporation. I am impressed by the way staff at all levels work as a team. I also appreciate how the company supports the community.

I have enclosed a copy of my resume. I would appreciate the chance to meet you for an interview. I will call you early next week to set up an appointment.

Thank you for your time.

Sincerely,

John Sewell

John Sewell

Enclosure

A Winning Cover Letter

Use a cover letter you have already written, or write a letter applying for one of the jobs in the activity on page 44. Check your letter. Have you followed these guidelines? If part of your letter needs more work, revise it. Then check the letter again.

Yes	Needs Work	
_____	_____	**1.** Address the letter to a specific person, including title, if possible.
_____	_____	**2.** State the position you are applying for.
_____	_____	**3.** Tell how you learned about the position you are applying for.
_____	_____	**4.** Briefly state why you are interested in the job.
_____	_____	**5.** Customize your letter to fit the job you are applying for.
_____	_____	**6.** Highlight one or two strong points from your experience.
_____	_____	**7.** Briefly show that your qualifications meet the job requirements.
_____	_____	**8.** Stress what you can offer the employer.
_____	_____	**9.** Don't include salary requirements.
_____	_____	**10.** Don't mention gaps in employment or other negatives.
_____	_____	**11.** Request an interview, and tell the person how to contact you.
_____	_____	**12.** Say that you will follow up with a phone call. Then do it.
_____	_____	**13.** Organize your information in no more than five brief paragraphs.
_____	_____	**14.** Use strong, precise wording.
_____	_____	**15.** Keep your letter brief and on one page.
_____	_____	**16.** Type the letter on paper that matches your resume.
_____	_____	**17.** State that your resume is enclosed. Put *Enclosure* at the bottom of the letter.
_____	_____	**18.** Carefully check spelling, punctuation, and capitalization.

Chapter 7
References

Most employers will ask you for references. They want to know how well you did in previous jobs. References are people who can tell them what kind of worker you are.

The best references are people you have worked for: your supervisor, a manager, or the owner of a company. People you have worked for in your last or current job are most important.

Other good choices are people from previous jobs or people who know you in private life. You might pick a neighbor, a teacher, or a coworker. (It's not a good idea to use relatives, though.) You should plan to have at least three references.

You've already listed possible references on your personal information sheet (see Chapter 4). Try to choose people with good things to say about you. Then call them and ask if they are willing to be references.

If they agree, tell them what jobs you are applying for. If you need to, remind them of any of your success stories they could talk about.

When you ask for references, it gets the word out that you are looking for a job. One of your references may pass your name on to other people. Another may tell you about a job opening where she works.

List your references on a separate sheet of paper. Try to use the same paper as you used for your resume and cover letters. Put your name and the word *References* at the top. For each reference, include

- first and last names, spelled correctly.
- telephone number and address at which the person can be reached. If he may be called at work, give the name of the company.
- position or title.
- how the person knows you.

Be sure not to include anyone on your reference list unless the person has agreed.

You do not need to give any references until you are asked. This may happen at a job interview. Or you may be asked to supply references before an interview is scheduled.

Francis Chisolm   *References*

William Smolka
Production Manager
Metal Artistry, Inc.
Industrial Parkway East
Springfield, AR 45543
(501) 555-5457
Mr. Smolka was my supervisor for 10 years.

Making a Reference List

Create a draft of your reference list by filling out the blanks below.

_____ *References*
  (your name)

1. Name:_____ Job title:_____

Business address:_____

Daytime phone number:_____

How the person knows you:_____

2. Name:_____ Job title:_____

Business address:_____

Daytime phone number:_____

How the person knows you:_____

3. Name:_____ Job title:_____

Business address:_____

Daytime phone number:_____

How the person knows you: _____

Chapter 8
Want Ads and Employment Agencies

There are four main ways to look for jobs:

- answering ads
- applying to employment agencies
- networking
- using target letters and direct contacts

This chapter talks about the first two ways. Many people find these the easiest ways to use. They know that a company is hiring. Ads or employment agencies can provide a lot of information:

- what the job is
- what qualifications the employer wants
- some of the working conditions (for example, hours, pay, etc.)
- how to apply
- deadline for applying

But ads and employment agencies have some drawbacks, too. Competition is intense. Only one-third of all job openings are ever advertised. Still, many people are successful, if they keep trying.

Answering Ads

Many people look in the newspaper for job ads. Don't forget other sources. One is the Internet. More and more jobs are posted there. Many public libraries have computers you can use to check the Internet. Library workers can show you how to find useful job ads. The activity on page 43 mentions helpful places to look for job ads.

When you find an ad that interests you, read it to see how to apply. The ad should tell you to call, come in person, or send information. In the activity on page 44, you practice looking at two job ads. It lets you think about what the ads tell you and how you would answer them.

Where to Start Looking

Identify sources of job information that you can use. Write the information on this form. Continue your list on separate paper if necessary.

Newspapers (classified or help wanted ads)

Name of newspaper(s): _____

Section(s) in classified ads to check (Sales, Health Care, Computers, etc.):

_____

Internet

Web site(s): _____

Other online resource(s): _____

Government Agencies (state labor department, city or county job agencies, etc.)

Agency: _____   Phone: _____

Address: _____   Hours: _____

Library Resources (job listings, phone books, computers for Internet access, etc.)

Library: _____   Address: _____

Resources: _____

School Placement Office (bulletin boards, counseling for students or alumni, etc.)

School: _____   Address: _____

Resources: _____

Bulletin Boards (in government offices, union offices, companies, stores, etc.)

Location: _____

Location: _____

Read each job ad. Answer the questions that follow it. On separate paper, write two questions you would ask to get more information about that job.

> DATA ENTRY Approx. 20-25 hrs./wk. $10.00/hr.
> Some experience pref. Must type 35 wpm.
> Call Mrs. Evans, 555-9212 8:30-4 to schedule an interview.

1. What do the following abbreviations mean?

   a. Approx. _____   **c.** pref. _____

   b. hrs./wk. _____   **d.** wpm _____

2. Is this a full-time or part-time job? What tells you that? _____

3. **a.** What qualifications does the job require? _____

   b. What qualifications are desired? _____

4. What should you do to apply for this job? _____

> ENGINEERING DEPT. A/C Tech opening. Elec. knowledge
> a must; A/C certificate a plus. Some evenings and week-
> ends. Fax resume and salary req. ASAP to 555-6398. EOE

1. What do the following abbreviations mean?

   a. DEPT. _____   **d.** Elec. _____

   b. A/C _____   **e.** req. _____

   c. Tech _____   **f.** EOE _____

2. **a.** What qualifications does the job require? _____

   b. What qualifications are desired? _____

3. What should you do to apply for this job? _____

4. If you applied, what would you say about salaries? _____

Applying by phone

Some ads will give a phone number to call. Before you pick up the phone, prepare yourself.

- Read the ad carefully.
- Underline what the employer wants.
- Have your personal information sheet or resume handy so you can answer questions.
- Smile—then pick up the phone.

Here's an example of an ad:

This employer wants experience, your own transportation, and a clean driving record.

Here's how this call might go:

"My name is _____. I am calling about your recent ad for cleaners. Am I talking to the right person?

"I have worked as a cleaner for two years with the XY Company. I have good references. I also have a car and a clean driving record.

"I'm available immediately. I could stop by at your convenience for an interview. When would be a good time for you?

"Could you tell me the name and address of your company? Who should I ask for when I arrive?"

When you call, some companies may ask you to send your resume. Be sure to ask for the name of the person to send it to, and ask for the correct spelling of the name. Send your resume with a one-page cover letter. (See Chapter 6 on writing cover letters.) Be sure to mention the phone conversation in your letter.

Applying in person

Some ads will ask you to apply in person. Here's an example:

Take your personal information sheet and your resume with you. It's important to prepare for the meeting. Read Chapter 12 and practice answering interview questions before you go.

Applying by letter

Some companies ask you to apply in writing. You should send your resume with a cover letter. Include any other materials (such as references) the ad asks for. See Chapter 6 for a sample cover letter answering a newspaper ad.

Employment Agencies and Temporary Work

Many companies use employment agencies. The agencies keep lists of available workers and propose the best ones to companies. The company decides who to hire.

Most employment agencies handle both temporary and permanent jobs. If you are offered a temporary job, you can ask if it might lead to a permanent one.

You can apply to employment agencies by answering their ads in the paper. You can also find employment agencies in the yellow pages of the phone book. (Check headings such as "Employment Agencies" or "Employment Contractors—Temporary Help.") Be sure to check your state employment service too. It has job listings for your entire state.

You can call an agency or state office and ask how to apply. You can also contact them by going in person with your resume.

Employment agencies will interview you, and they may test your skills. If a suitable job comes up, they refer you to an employer. The employer makes the hiring decision.

Look for fee-paid employment agencies. This means the agency is paid by the employer. You will not have to pay anything.

Because employment agencies are paid by the employer, they work for the employer. They won't look for a job for you. It's not a good idea to use only agencies in looking for work. If you try some other ideas in this book too, you're more likely to get a job.

If you can't visit an employment agency, you can send a cover letter and your resume. Call first to ask who should get your letter, and the correct spelling of the name.

Page 47 shows a sample letter to an agency.

Ernest Holcomb
145 School Street
West Valley, PA 19674
(717) 555-9876

November 16, 2000

Ms. Adele Pearson
Pearson Employment Agency
1919 Sixth Street
East Valley, PA 19763

Dear Ms. Pearson:

I am looking for a manufacturing job as a shop floor worker. As you will see from my resume, I have eight years' experience in manufacturing.

My special skills are
- sheet metal work
- operation of punch presses, lathes, and other machines
- tool maintenance
- building maintenance (doors, windows, plumbing, painting, etc.)

I am a fast and reliable worker. I am looking for a stable job but would accept temporary work, especially if it could lead to a permanent position.

My last pay rate was $10.50 per hour.

I would be glad to meet with you at your convenience. I'll call you early next week to arrange a time.

Sincerely,

Ernest Holcomb

Ernest Holcomb

Enclosure

Chapter 9
Networking and Direct Contacts

Many people find jobs through ads and agencies. But many more succeed with the other two strategies:

- networking
- using target letters and direct contacts

Networking

In Chapter 3, you started a networking list. Now, contact some of the people on the list. Start with those you know well. Tell them you are looking for a job. Ask their advice (but don't expect them to get you a job).

☞ It's helpful to work at expanding your networking circle. You might start a volunteer activity or get more active in the PTA. You can also ask your networking contacts who else you should talk to.

You might say:

- "You've probably heard I'm looking for work. I have a new resume. I'd like to show it to you and see what you think about it."
- "I'm looking for a job. I'm considering the restaurant or hotel industry. I'd like to find out what you know. Can we get together so I can get some advice and ideas from you?"

You did not ask these people to find you a job. You asked them for advice.

As you talk to your networking contacts, make notes about what happens. The activity on page 49 shows one way to do this. You can use additional paper for notes about more contacts. Or you can use index cards—one card for each person.

Review the networking list you started in Chapter 3. Select the people you want to contact. Use the form below to plan the contacts and record the results. Use more paper for additional contacts. You can also use one index card for each person.

Person: _____ Phone number: _____

Before: Best way to contact: _____ phone call _____ meeting

Questions to ask: _____

_____

After: Results: _____

Date of contact:_____ _____ Sent thank-you letter

Person: _____ Phone number: _____

Before: Best way to contact: _____ phone call _____ meeting

Questions to ask: _____

_____

After: Results: _____

Date of contact:_____ _____ Sent thank-you letter

Person: _____ Phone number: _____

Before: Best way to contact: _____ phone call _____ meeting

Questions to ask: _____

_____

After: Results: _____

Date of contact:_____ _____ Sent thank-you letter

The Networking Meeting

The networking meeting is a more formal kind of networking. In a networking meeting, you want to

- let the person know that you are looking for a job
- get information and advice
- get the names of other people who may be able to help

The chart below shows some questions that a job seeker might ask in a networking meeting.

- Here is my resume. What do you think of it? Do you have any suggestions for improving it? If you read it, would you give me an interview?

- I plan to apply for a job as _____. Do you think this kind of position is right for me, or do you think I should apply for another kind of job?

- I'm thinking about working in the _____ industry. Do you think that is a good idea? Do you know any good companies in this industry? Do you know anyone else who may know something about this industry?

- I saw an ad for a job at the _____ company, and I plan to apply. Do you know anything about this company? Do you know anybody who works there?

- Do you think your employer could use someone with my skills? In what kind of position? How should I go about applying? Can you give me an introduction? What is the name of the person I should contact?

- On my job search, I'm answering ads, contacting employment agencies, and using whatever contacts I have. Can you suggest anything else I could do?

- How did you find your job?

- I want to approach some employment agencies. Can you recommend any?

- Do you know anyone else I could contact for more information? Can I tell that person you referred me?

Your specific questions will vary depending on

- who your contact is
- how well you know your contact
- what information your contact has

In a networking meeting, the conversation can be friendly and informal. But don't use more time than you need.

Target Letters and Direct Contacts

As you know, most jobs are filled without ads or an employment agency. This section talks about how to contact companies directly.

The flowchart to the right shows the steps in the usual hiring process at a large company.

It may take months for a company to get to the external search. And if the in-company search finds a good candidate, the external search may never happen.

When you make direct contact, you want to get to a manager who has the problem described in the flowchart. If the manager sees you as a possible solution, she may skip steps and invite you for an interview.

With this approach, you won't have a lot of competition. In fact, you may be the only candidate.

How do you find the manager who has the problem? It's not easy. The best way is through networking.

Another way is through trial and error. Call each company on your company list. Ask the switchboard operator to tell you who manages the department you're interested in. Do not say that you are looking for a job, or

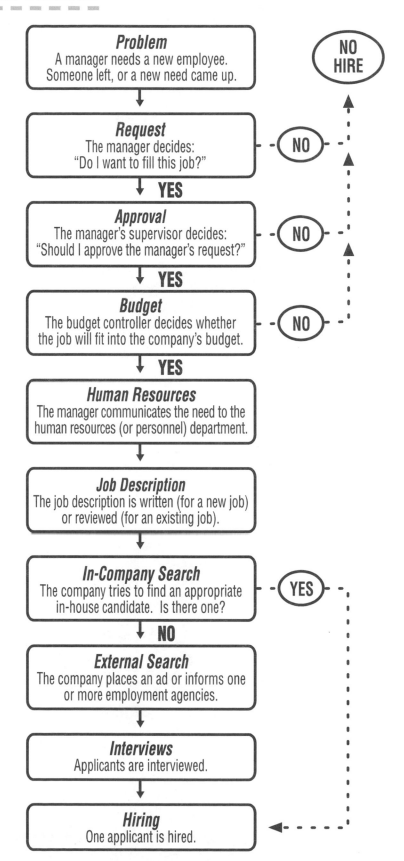

the operator will refer you to human resources. You could say something like this:

"I need to write a letter to the head of your _____ division. Could you please give me the correct spelling of the name? What's his correct title? And the address?"

Now you have two choices:

Use the phone

Call the person you found out about. Explain who you are and what you can do. Use a "commercial" that you prepare beforehand to sell your skills and experience. (See page 64.) Ask for an interview. You could say something like this:

"Mr. Miller, my name is Joe Fowler. May I have a moment of your time? I am an experienced mechanic, trained in using most power tools and tooling machines. Would you have any use for somebody with my skills? I can come by with my resume if that would be convenient for you."

Write a target letter

A target letter is a letter you send to a company you're interested in. Send it to the person in charge of the department you want to work for. Do not enclose your resume. (If a resume is included, the letter may be directed to the human resources department. The person you want to reach may never read it.)

A short letter has the best chance of being read. Page 53 shows an example.

Your target letter is important because you will send it out to many different companies. Take some time over it. Keep coming back to it until you are satisfied that this is the best letter you can write.

Frank Henwood
12 Sea Road
Upville, NY 12045
(345) 555-8990

April 12, 2000

Mr. Jake Smith
Jake's Auto Repair
1122 Pearl Street
Downtown, NY 12433

Dear Mr. Smith,

I am an experienced auto mechanic and am looking for a new position. I have training and expertise in maintenance and repair of foreign and domestic cars and trucks.

I worked for six years at Auto City. I performed state inspections and all kinds of repairs. I also often dealt with customers. I was laid off when the company downsized.

My responsibilities included supervising the work of two other mechanics. I also reorganized our parts inventory system. As a result, there were fewer delays, the shop saved money, and the customers were more satisfied.

I would appreciate having a chance to talk with you. I'll give you a call next week to arrange a meeting.

Sincerely,

Frank Henwood

Frank Henwood

Limit how many target letters you send out each week, because you'll want to follow up on all of them. Five to seven days after sending each letter, call the person on the phone.

This phone call is your key to success. When managers read a letter, they may be interested but too busy to deal with it, so they put the letter aside. But if you call, the manager may be happy to talk to you and keep you in mind for any openings, now or later.

When you call the person you addressed the letter to, say something like this:

"Mr. Smith, this is Frank Henwood. I wrote you a letter a few days ago, offering my services as a mechanic. Did you receive my letter? Would it be possible for me to come by and meet you?"

You cannot always expect to reach the person you want with your first call. You may have to call a busy person three or more times. But do not give up—keep at it.

Do not talk to anybody else. Just say something like this:

"I wrote him a letter a few days ago and wanted to make an appointment. I think I have to talk to him directly. When do you think is a good time to reach him?"

Then try to call again. Your goal is to be invited for an interview or asked to submit a resume.

The activity on page 55 gives you a checklist for using target letters. You can use it to help you keep your job hunt on track.

Do not get discouraged. The next try may be the successful one!

Target Letter Checklist

Use this checklist to keep your target letters on track.

Step 1: Find managers who may need a new employee.

   _____ Talk to networking contacts.

   _____ Review your company list. Call each company's switchboard.

   _____ Ask for the managers' names, titles, addresses, and phone numbers.

Step 2: Get ready to contact the managers.

   _____ Prepare short target letter.

   _____ Prepare "commercial" to use in phone calls.

Step 3: Begin contacting the managers.

   _____ Begin sending target letters.

   _____ DON'T include your resume.

   _____ Limit the number of target letters so you can follow up.

Step 4: Follow up.

   _____ Follow up on each letter with a phone call.

   _____ Keep trying till you reach the person you want.

   _____ Ask for an interview.

   _____ Don't get discouraged!

Chapter 10
Staying Organized

You may have to make 100 contacts or more before you find a job. It's a good idea to follow a plan and keep records of your contacts, letters, and phone calls. If you are organized and stay on top of the facts, it will make a good impression on employers.

Keeping Records

You'll want to keep written records for all your networking contacts and for every company you research.

For each contact, be sure to keep track of

- the contact's name
- what was said
- when the conversation took place
- any letters you or your contact wrote
- any follow-up you need to do

The best way is to take notes. Many people find index cards the most practical. You can carry them with you and make notes right after a meeting.

Page 57 shows four examples of index cards. Two cards are for networking contacts. The others are for companies. In the "Action" column, *P* means phone call and *M* means meeting.

Networking File Cards

Front

Chang, Barbara
Hilltop Apartments, Apt. 4-A, Terre Haute, IN 50301
Home phone: unlisted

Personnel Manager
ABC Company
1329 River Blvd., Terre Haute, IN 50312
Business phone: (812) 555-3136

Remarks: Got her name from Alex's father at PTA meeting

Back

Date	Action	Summary	Next Step
2/10	P	Agreed to see me	2/15, PM
2/15	M	30-minute meeting. Gave me two names; made file cards for them.	Write thank-you letter.

Front

Brennan, Louis
12 Elm Street, Hilltop, OR 96432

Head Teller
City Bank
1440 Main Street, Hilltop, OR 96427
Business phone: 555-7243

Remarks:

Back

Date	Action	Summary	Next Step
5/14	M	Met him in line at post office; said to call next week.	5/20, AM
5/20	P	Thinks bank will be hiring soon— said to keep in touch.	Call again in early June.

Company File Cards

Front

ABC Company
1329 River Blvd., Terre Haute, IN 50312
(812) 555-3100 (switchboard)

Important people:
    Chang, Barbara, Personnel Manager
    Sumner, John, Production Manager

Main products: circuit boards

Other information:
See Web site: http://www.xxxxxx.xxx

Back

Date	Action	Contacts	What happened	Next action
9/11	P	John Sumner	Will see me.	Call 9/16.
9/16	P	John Sumner	No decision yet; will call me next week.	Call 9/27.

Front

City Bank
1440 Main Street, Hilltop, OR 96427
555-7200 (switchboard)

Important people:
    Brennan, Louis, Head Teller

Type of business:
    local commercial bank

Other information:
Town history at library has story of bank's founding.

Back

Date	Action	Contacts	What happened	Next action
5/20	P	Louis Brennan	Said to keep in touch— may be hiring soon.	Call in early June.

A Weekly Job Search Plan

A job search plan will also help you stay organized. And it will help you keep up the pace of your job search.

How much time you can spend on your job search depends on other things in your life. Only you can decide how much time you can put into your job search.

A sample weekly plan appears below. It shows a good level of activity for someone who can look for work full-time. A job seeker might reach this level two or three weeks after starting the job search.

Weekly Plan for an Active Job Search

Phone calls

for networking meetings 5
to target companies. 10
to employment agencies 3
to answer ads in newspapers and other listings 10

Total **28**

Letters

to answer ads in newspapers and other listings 5
target letters 10
thank-you letters after networking
    meetings or interviews 5

Total **20**

Meetings

networking meetings 3
job interviews. 4

Total **7**

Total activities for the week **55**

Chapter 11
The Application Form

When you apply for a job, many companies ask you to fill in an application form. This gives them much of the basic information they need about you. Every company has a different form, but most of the questions are the same.

The information you need for an application form is on the personal information sheet you created in Chapter 4. Whenever you visit an employer, take your personal information sheet with you. That way, you'll have all the information you need.

Messy forms make a bad impression. Try to get two copies of any application form. If you can, take the form home and bring it back later. Take the time to complete the form carefully.

Use one copy of the form for a first draft. Do it in pencil so you can make corrections. Then copy the answers onto the second form.

When you fill in an application form, be sure to do the following:

- Print neatly in blue or black ink.
- Read the whole form carefully before you begin. Read it again after you finish to make sure it's complete.
- If you don't understand a question, ask the person who gave you the form to explain.
- Double-check names, dates, telephone numbers, and addresses you write.

Answer every question on an application form. If a question doesn't apply to you, write "Does not apply." If you want to explain an answer, write "Will discuss in interview."

Remember that the information you give may be checked. If you give false answers, you may not be hired. If you get the job, you could lose it if the employer finds out later that you didn't tell the truth.

Illegal Questions

Some questions are illegal. You don't have to answer questions on these topics on an application form or in an interview:

- your age or date of birth
- your race
- arrests (An employer can ask if you've ever been convicted of a crime, though.)
- number of children or childcare arrangements
- handicaps
- your marital status (single, married, separated, or divorced)
- your religion or what religious holidays you observe
- your sex
- your sexual orientation

Chapter 12
The Job Interview

Your contacts, cover letter, and resume help you get an interview. An interview helps you get the job. You'll want to have good interview skills and prepare ahead of time.

The Basics of the Job Interview

In an interview, an employer wants to find out if you can do the job and if you'll fit in. You want to find out if you like the job and can do it. You also want to make a good impression.

It's a good idea to practice for an interview. You can do this by yourself or with someone else. Practice answering the questions you might be asked. Some common interview questions are on page 66. The activities on pages 65, 67 and 70 can also help you prepare.

Basic Guidelines for Interviews

Here are some important guidelines for interviews. Following them will help you make a good impression.
- Be on time.
- Go by yourself.
- Be confident about your skills, training, and experience.
- Take with you your resume, personal information sheet, and any other documents you've been asked for.
- Prepare yourself well for every interview. What do you know about the job? What do you know about the company? The more you know in advance, the better your chances are of getting the job.
- Avoid tight, revealing clothes.
- Avoid too much perfume or cologne.
- Don't wear too much makeup or flashy jewelry.
- Dress suitably for the job—the way you would dress for work or a little better. Conservative business clothes are better than casual, trendy styles.
- Don't overdress. For example, don't wear a suit and tie to apply for a construction job.

- Personal grooming is important. Make sure your clothes are neat, clean, and in good repair.
- Make sure your hair and nails are neat and clean.
- Make sure your shoes are polished.
- Don't smoke.
- Don't chew gum or tobacco.
- Don't ramble. Give short, precise answers, not long explanations. Stick to the topic. (When you practice, keep your answers to two minutes or shorter. But don't look at your watch in the interview.)
- Talk about yourself only to show how you could do the job and benefit the company.
- Listen carefully before answering questions.
- Ask questions about the job, not about pay and benefits. Don't talk about pay and benefits unless you are offered a job or are asked a question about them. Then, don't ask for more pay than the job is worth.
- Listen carefully to the answers to your questions.
- Never bad-mouth your former employers or supervisors. The interviewer may think that you are a difficult person. Be positive, even if you have bad feelings.
- Don't make excuses for yourself in a previous job.
- Keep a positive attitude.
- Smile.
- Focus on traits that make anyone a good employee: work well with people; communicate clearly; use a computer; work well on a team; good at solving problems; loyal and honest.

The first impression you make is very important. These things can help:

- Come through the door with your head up.
- Look at the interviewer and introduce yourself.
- Be ready for a handshake, but don't hold out your hand. The interviewer may not like to shake hands.
- If you do shake hands, do so firmly.
- Wait until you're asked before sitting.
- Make good eye contact with the interviewer during the interview.
- Don't make too much eye contact. Staring can make the interviewer nervous.
- Be friendly but professional. Keep a businesslike attitude.

DO   **DON'T**

Your "Commercial"

Interviewers often start an interview by saying, "Tell me something about yourself."

This is your chance to sell yourself.

When you have the chance to talk freely, don't simply repeat your resume. Focus on your strong points.

A good way to do this is to mention four points: the job you can do, your skills, your experience, and your character. You can also talk about your education or other topics. But mention only things that could be important in your job.

Below is a sample "commercial."

"Commercial"

JOB:

"I **am a** carpenter and became a specialist in building maintenance."

SKILLS:

"I **am good at** constantly checking on buildings and doing all the repairs, such as plumbing, hanging drywall, carpentry, and fixing locks and lights. I am also experienced in supervising outside contractors."

EXPERIENCE:

"**In my last job** I maintained two buildings and ensured that a major repair of the roofs was finished by the contractors on time and under budget."

CHARACTER:

"I **am** responsible, reliable, and easy to work with. I've always had pleasant relationships with my superiors, my coworkers, and the contractors. I can be firm when necessary."

It is a good idea to write your "commercial" and practice it ahead of time. It should take one minute to two minutes—no longer.

Preparing Your Own Commercial

Prepare to tell an interviewer about yourself. Complete the sentences. If you wish, add other information that can impress an employer. Then practice saying your "commercial" out loud.

Job

I am a(n) _____

I want to _____

Skills

I can _____

I know how to _____

I am also good at _____

Experience

In my last job I _____

My responsibilities included _____

I have also _____

Character

I am _____

In my relationships with other people, I _____

Goals

I am applying for this job because _____

I believe I can contribute to the company by _____

I hope that I can _____

Questions You May Be Asked

During the interview, the interviewer will ask you questions about yourself or about other jobs you've had. Some of the questions are not easy to answer. You need to prepare and practice clear answers before you go to a job interview.

Common interview questions

- Why do you want to work for this company?
- What do you know about this company?
- Describe your ideal working environment.
- What do you look for in a job?
- What are your three greatest strengths?
- In your career so far, what do you think is your greatest success?
- What are your goals? Where do you see yourself in five years?
- What kind of work interests you?
- Do you have any special training or skills?
- Do you work well under pressure?
- Would you be willing to relocate?
- Are you willing to work extra hours when needed?
- How do you deal with stress?
- What do you like to do in your spare time?
- How would you describe your personality?
- What are the qualities of a good supervisor?
- What did you like most about your last job?
- What were your duties on your last job?
- How does your experience relate to this job?
- Why do you want this job?
- Why are you the best candidate for the job?
- How long would you keep this job?
- How would other people describe you?
- How do you get along with your coworkers?
- How did you get along with your last supervisor?
- If I called your last supervisor and asked for a recommendation, what would she say?
- Do you have any questions?
- When can you start?

The Complete

Interview Questions

Write your answers to these common interview questions. Then practice saying them out loud.

1. What are your strengths?

   _____

2. How would your last supervisor describe your work?

   _____

3. What do you feel is your greatest success?

   _____

4. What did you like most about your last job?

   _____

5. How do you get along with your coworkers?

   _____

6. What were your major responsibilities in your last job?

   _____

7. How can you contribute to this company?

   _____

8. What are your goals? What do you want to be doing in five years?

   _____

9. Tell me about your hobbies, any volunteer work you do, and so on.

   _____

Dealing with Difficult Questions

In some interviews, you may be asked difficult questions. Try to predict what questions might be difficult for you. Decide ahead of time how you will answer them.

Never lie—you could lose the job if you do. But try to deal with these questions in the most positive way you can.

Here are some examples of difficult questions and possible answers.

Question:

"Why did you leave your last job?"

Possible Answers:
- "The company downsized, and I was laid off."
- "I wanted to find a position with more room for growth."
- If you were fired for personal reasons, try to put a positive spin on it. For example, "The department was reorganized, and my duties changed. I wanted to find a job where I could work more independently." Never say "I couldn't stand my boss" or "I didn't get along with my coworkers." Don't blame someone else if you had job troubles.

Question:

"Why did they choose to lay you off and not someone else?"

Possible Answers:
- "I'd been there the shortest time."
- "My whole department was eliminated."
- "They only kept people who had experience in sales, which I didn't."

Question:

"What are your weaknesses?"

Possible Answer:
- See Chapter 1. Try to mention a weakness that's also a strength. For example, "I am sometimes too fussy about details. On the other hand, my boss could always be sure that my work was carefully done."

Question:

"You were with the same company for twenty-one years. Can you still adapt to new situations?"

Possible Answer:

- "There were many changes in the company during this time. In the last six years I had four supervisors, and the company had two owners. I always adapted well."

Question:

"You don't have quite enough experience in some areas. Why do you think you'll be able to do this job?"

Possible Answer:

- "I'm a fast learner. I'm willing and eager to learn. If there are any classes you think I should take, I'll be happy to."

Question:

"How much do you want to earn?"

Possible Answer:

- Try not to give a direct answer. Instead, try to find out what they are willing to pay: "What have you planned to pay for this job?"

Question:

"What did you dislike about your last job?"

Possible Answer:

- Use the list you made in Chapter 1. Mention only one thing, and make it short. For example: "They didn't have enough work to keep me busy."

Question:

"You left your last job nine months ago. Why didn't you find a job sooner?"

Possible Answers:

Do not give the impression that you have been doing nothing. Say something like:

- "I've been working hard to find a good job, but the job market is very tight."
- "I relocated, and it's taken some time to find possible jobs in a new city."

Write your answers to these interview questions, which may be difficult. Then practice saying them out loud.

1. What are your weaknesses?

_____

2. Why did you leave your last job? *or* Why do you want to leave your current job?

_____

3. You don't seem to have much experience/training in this field.

_____

4. You've changed jobs a lot, haven't you? *or* You've been out of work a long time.

_____

5. Have you ever been convicted of a crime?

_____

6. Have you ever been fired or laid off from a job? Why?

_____

7. How much do you expect to earn?

_____

8. How well did you get along with your last supervisor?

_____

9. What responsibilities do you have that might interfere with your work?

_____

Questions You May Want to Ask

After interviewers ask their questions, most will ask if you have any questions. If this doesn't happen, at the end of the interview you can say, "May I ask you some questions?" You want to gather enough information to decide if you want the job.

It's best to prepare good questions ahead of time. Your questions may change from interview to interview. (See below for some examples.)

Sample Questions to Ask in an Interview

- Can you tell me more about the company?
- Is this a new position, or would I replace someone?
- What exactly are the job duties?
- What are the working hours? Will there be overtime?
- Who would my supervisor be?
- Can I do anything to prepare myself for the job before starting?

Sample Questions to Ask When You're Offered a Job

- What have you planned to pay for this job?
- Will you cover my health insurance? How about my family?
- Do you have a retirement plan? Can I join it right away? What would I contribute?
- When would you like me to start?

Write down your questions so you don't forget any. Don't be afraid to take out your notes during the interview. It shows the interviewer that you came well prepared.

The End of the Interview

The interviewer may not give you an answer on the spot because the company wants to interview other candidates. If you're told "We'll let you know," ask, "When can I expect to hear from you?" Make a note of the answer.

Before you leave, thank the person who interviewed you. Be sure to get the names (with correct spellings) of the interviewer and anyone else who helped you.

After the Interview

Write a thank-you letter to the interviewer the same day or early the next day. Also write to anyone else who helped you. Say that you are still interested in the job. Take this chance to mention your strong points again.

Page 73 shows a sample thank-you letter.

If you don't hear from the company, follow up with a phone call. Be friendly and businesslike. Say something like, "I spoke to you about the _____ position last week. You thought you'd have an answer for me by yesterday. I wanted to check on the status of the position."

If the company hasn't decided yet, ask when they expect to decide. Follow up again on that date if you haven't heard.

Thank-You Letter

Laura Fitzgerald
200 West Lake Street
Hicksville, NY 11801

June 14, 2000

Mr. Howard Osada
Fairmount Industries
58 East Avenue
Astoria, NY 11160

Dear Mr. Osada,

I would like to thank you for taking the time to talk with me about the office manager position today. I was happy to discuss how I would fit into the team at Fairmount Industries.

I was struck by how I'd be able to help with keeping the office organized and the work flowing. My experience in juggling priorities and working under pressure would be useful in such a busy company. I feel sure I could be an asset to Fairmount Industries.

You mentioned that you expect to make a decision next week. I look forward to speaking with you then. Please feel free to call me if you have any more questions.

Sincerely,

Laura Fitzgerald

Laura Fitzgerald

Getting Ready for the Interview

This checklist will help you prepare for a job interview.

Prepare for the interview ahead of time.

_____ Learn about the company. Some places you can look: the company's web site, the public library, newspaper clippings, trade associations, the Chamber of Commerce, the Better Business Bureau. You can also ask the company for written information.

_____ Ask your friends if they know anyone who works for the company.

_____ Learn about the job. If you can, get a copy of the job description when you schedule the interview.

_____ Practice your answers to common interview questions. Stick to two minutes or less.

_____ Learn how to pronounce the interviewer's name before you meet.

The night before the interview, get your clothes ready and collect other things you'll need.

_____ Choose conservative clothes suitable for the job. Make sure they're clean, pressed, and in good repair.

_____ Polish your shoes.

_____ Don't plan to wear flashy makeup or jewelry.

_____ Take a briefcase or folder.

_____ Take a pencil or pen, a notebook or writing pad, and an appointment calendar.

_____ Take your personal information sheet and any other documents you'll need. Bring several copies of your resume.

_____ Take a list of questions you want to ask the interviewer.

The day of the interview:

_____ Use deodorant. Wear little or no perfume or cologne.

_____ Be sure your hands and hair are clean and neat.

_____ Dress appropriately for the weather.

_____ Don't eat garlic or spicy foods before an interview.

_____ Don't drink alcohol before an interview.

_____ Leave yourself plenty of time. Plan to arrive at least 10 minutes early.

Chapter 13

Getting the Best Pay and Conditions

If you are offered a job, now is your chance to discuss pay, benefits, and working conditions.

Sometimes there is nothing to discuss or negotiate. For some jobs, the company tells you what your duties, pay, and benefits will be. You take it or leave it.

But on many jobs there is room for some negotiation. When an employer really wants you, he may be willing to improve on the first offer.

It is worth asking for better pay or benefits, but don't ask for more than the job is worth. Keep in mind that your requests must make sense for the employer, or you won't get them. See page 76 for an activity to help you practice.

Here is a checklist of points to consider:

Money	Other Benefits	Relocation	Job Description
• salary/pay	• insurance: medical, disability, dental, life	• moving cost	• place of work
• commissions	• vacation	• temporary housing	• supervisor
• bonus	• retirement plan	• help in selling your home	• duties
	• educational programs	• bridge loan to transfer mortgage	

☞ What if you don't know what the job is worth? Maybe someone on your networking list would know better.

Not likely to work

"I want more money."

More likely to work

"I think with my experience I am worth a bit more. You won't have to train me, and I'll be productive from day one. Don't you think that's worth $_____ more?"

Talking about Pay and Benefits

Imagine you've been offered a job. Now you're discussing pay and benefits with the employer. Which statements are most likely to help you get what you want?

Employer: "How much money do you want to make?"

____ "I want $_____."

____ "What is the pay range for this job?"

Employer: "Why should we pay you that much?"

____ "I have lots of bills to pay."

____ "I have lots of experience. I'll be a productive worker."

Employer: "The pay offer is firm. We can't give you more money."

____ "But I think I'm worth more."

____ "Would you consider a salary review after six months? By then, I'll have shown you how valuable I am."

Employer: "You'll get health insurance after six months."

____ "I think you should give me health insurance right away."

____ "If I pay the premium, can I get insurance right away?"

In each case, the second statement is a better choice. They speak in a way that will make sense to the employer. What other statements might help you get the best possible pay and benefits? Note your ideas below:

_____

_____

_____

_____

_____

_____

_____

Here's a sample story. Maria was offered a job. She was told that she would make $7.20 per hour and that she could start next Monday. Then she began her negotiation:

Maria: There is one point I would like to clarify. Could you explain the health insurance plan? Is my family included?

Supervisor: You will be covered right away, but your family only after three months.

Maria: This is really a problem for me. It would be difficult for me to find my family coverage for the next three months. Can you cover them from day one if I pay a part of the premium?

Supervisor: I think that should be possible, but you may have to pay the whole premium. I'll talk with Human Resources about it.

Maria: Thank you very much. Could we do this right now?

The Human Resources manager said Maria would have to pay the premium for three months. But she got what she needed: family insurance right away.

Chapter 14
Tips for Your New Job

Congratulations! The work of looking for a job is over for now. Here are some tips for getting off to a good start in your new job.

Be modest.

Follow the company's rules and procedures.
If you have new ideas, share them tactfully.
Try not to criticize your coworkers.

Use your first weeks well.

Your boss and coworkers will give you time to learn your new job. Ask lots of questions. It's better to ask questions than to make mistakes.

Don't be too afraid of mistakes.

Honest mistakes are part of learning. Don't be too hard on yourself. Admit your mistakes (and be sure not to repeat them).

Get to know key people.

Your boss and coworkers are key people for you. But other people in the company can also be key to your job. Get to know everyone who can help you do your work.

Show you have a good attitude.

Do your share or more.
Don't complain.
Learn about other parts of the company.
Keep your work area neat.
Look your best.

Be sure people can count on you.

Always do what you say you will.
Be helpful.
Volunteer for tasks no one else wants.

Earn your pay.

Do your work as well as you can.
Arrive on time (or early).
Leave on time (or late).

Enjoy your job.

Be friendly to your coworkers (but don't waste lots of time chatting).
Have fun.
Use humor.

Don't expect to stay forever.

There is no job security anymore. A takeover, a failing product, or another event may force the company to let you go.

Keep your eyes open for job possibilities. Make sure you stay employable. Keep your skills up to date.

Keep a list of your successes at work, big and small. Add to it each week. This list will give you a head start in planning your next job search.